PLEASE ENTER ON LOAN SLIP:

AUTHOR: STYRON, M.

TITLE: Darkness visible

ACCESSION NO: SA(N) 91473

DARKNESS
VISIBLE

DARKNESS VISIBLE

A
Memoir
of
Madness

WILLIAM
STYRON

JONATHAN CAPE
LONDON

First published in Great Britain 1991
Reprinted 1991 (three times)
Jonathan Cape Ltd, 20 Vauxhall Bridge Road, London SW1V 2SA
© William Styron 1990

Part of this work was originally
published in *Vanity Fair* in 1989

William Styron asserts his right to be
identified as the author of this work

A CIP catalogue record for this book
is available from the British Library

ISBN 0-224-03045-0

Printed in Great Britain by
Butler & Tanner Ltd, Frome and London

To Rose

This book began as a lecture given in Baltimore in May 1989 at a symposium on affective disorders sponsored by the Department of Psychiatry of The Johns Hopkins University School of Medicine. Greatly expanded, the text became an essay published in December of that year in *Vanity Fair*. I had originally intended to begin with a narrative of a trip I made to Paris—a trip which had special significance for me in terms of the development of the depressive illness from which I had suffered. But despite the exceptionally ample amount of space I was given by the magazine, there was an inevitable limit, and I had to discard this part in favor of other matters I wanted to deal with. In the present version, that section has been restored to its place at the beginning. Except for a few relatively minor changes and additions, the rest of the text remains as it originally appeared.

—W. S.

DARKNESS VISIBLE

For the thing which
I greatly feared is come upon me,
and that which I was afraid of
Is come unto me.
I was not in safety, neither
had I rest, neither was I quiet;
yet trouble came.

—Job

I

IN PARIS ON A CHILLY EVENING LATE IN OCTOBER OF
1985 I first became fully aware that the struggle with
the disorder in my mind—a struggle which had engaged me for several months—might have a fatal out-
come. The moment of revelation came as the car in
which I was riding moved down a rain-slick street not
far from the Champs-Élysées and slid past a dully glow-
ing neon sign that read HÔTEL WASHINGTON. I had not
seen that hotel in nearly thirty-five years, since the
spring of 1952, when for several nights it had become
my initial Parisian roosting place. In the first few
months of my *Wanderjahr*, I had come down to Paris by
train from Copenhagen, and landed at the Hôtel Washington through the whimsical determination of a New
York travel agent. In those days the hotel was one of the
many damp, plain hostelries made for tourists, chiefly
American, of very modest means who, if they were like
me—colliding nervously for the first time with the

French and their droll kinks—would always remember how the exotic bidet, positioned solidly in the drab bedroom, along with the toilet far down the ill-lit hallway, virtually defined the chasm between Gallic and Anglo-Saxon cultures. But I stayed at the Washington for only a short time. Within days I had been urged out of the place by some newly found young American friends who got me installed in an even seedier but more colorful hotel in Montparnasse, hard by Le Dôme and other suitably literary hangouts. (In my mid-twenties, I had just published a first novel and was a celebrity, though one of very low rank since few of the Americans in Paris had heard of my book, let alone read it.) And over the years the Hôtel Washington gradually disappeared from my consciousness.

It reappeared, however, that October night when I passed the gray stone façade in a drizzle, and the recollection of my arrival so many years before started flooding back, causing me to feel that I had come fatally full circle. I recall saying to myself that when I left Paris for New York the next morning it would be a matter of forever. I was shaken by the certainty with which I accepted the idea that I would never see France again, just as I would never recapture a lucidity that was slipping away from me with terrifying speed.

Only days before I had concluded that I was suffering from a serious depressive illness, and was floundering helplessly in my efforts to deal with it. I wasn't cheered by the festive occasion that had brought me to France. Of the many dreadful manifestations of the disease, both physical and psychological, a sense of self-hatred—or, put less categorically, a failure of self-esteem—is one of the most universally experienced symptoms, and I had suffered more and more from a general feeling of worthlessness as the malady had progressed. My dank joylessness was therefore all the more ironic because I had flown on a rushed four-day trip to Paris in order to accept an award which should have sparklingly restored my ego. Earlier that summer I received word that I had been chosen to receive the Prix Mondial Cino del Duca, given annually to an artist or scientist whose work reflects themes or principles of a certain "humanism." The prize was established in memory of Cino del Duca, an immigrant from Italy who amassed a fortune just before and after World War II by printing and distributing cheap magazines, principally comic books, though later branching out into publications of quality; he became proprietor of the newspaper *Paris-Jour*. He also produced movies and was a prominent racehorse owner, enjoying the pleasure of having many winners in France and abroad. Aiming for nobler cultural satisfactions, he evolved into a renowned philanthropist and along the way established a book-publishing firm that began to produce works of literary merit (by chance, my first novel, *Lie Down in Darkness,* was one of del Duca's offerings, in a translation entitled *Un Lit de Ténèbres*); by the time of his death in 1967 this house, Éditions Mondiales, became an important entity of a multifold empire that was rich yet prestigious enough for there to be scant memory of its comic-book origins when del Duca's widow, Simone, created a foundation whose chief function was the annual bestowal of the eponymous award.

The Prix Mondial Cino del Duca has become greatly respected in France—a nation pleasantly besotted with cultural prizegiving—not only for its eclecticism and the distinction shown in the choice of its recipients but for the openhandedness of the prize itself, which that year amounted to approximately $25,000. Among the winners during the past twenty years have been Konrad Lorenz, Alejo Carpentier, Jean Anouilh, Ignazio Silone, Andrei Sakharov, Jorge Luis Borges and one American, Lewis Mumford. (No women as yet, feminists take note.) As an American, I found it especially hard not to feel honored by inclusion in their company. While the giving and receiving of prizes usually induce from all sources an unhealthy uprising of false modesty, backbiting, self-torture and envy, my own view is that certain awards, though not necessary, can be very nice to receive. The Prix del Duca was to me so straightforwardly nice that any extensive self-examination seemed silly, and so I accepted gratefully, writing in reply that I would honor the reasonable requirement that I be present for the ceremony. At that time I looked forward to a leisurely trip, not a hasty turnaround. Had I been able to foresee my state of mind as the date of the award approached, I would not have accepted at all.

Depression is a disorder of mood, so mysteriously painful and elusive in the way it becomes known to the self—to the mediating intellect—as to verge close to being beyond description. It thus remains nearly incomprehensible to those who have not experienced it in its extreme mode, although the gloom, "the blues" which people go through occasionally and associate with the general hassle of everyday existence are of such prevalence that they do give many individuals a hint of the illness in its catastrophic form. But at the time of which I write I had descended far past those familiar, manageable doldrums. In Paris, I am able to see now, I was at a critical stage in the development of the disease, situated at an ominous way station between its unfocused stirrings earlier that summer and the near-violent denouement of December, which sent me into the hospital. I will later attempt to describe the evolution of this malady, from its earliest origins to my eventual hospitalization and recovery, but the Paris trip has retained a notable meaning for me.

On the day of the award ceremony, which was to take place at noon and be followed by a formal luncheon, I woke up at midmorning in my room at the Hôtel Pont-Royal commenting to myself that I felt reasonably sound, and I passed the good word along to my wife, Rose. Aided by the minor tranquilizer Halcion, I had managed to defeat my insomnia and get a few hours' sleep. Thus I was in fair spirits. But such wan cheer was an habitual pretense which I knew meant very little, for I was certain to feel ghastly before nightfall. I had come to a point where I was carefully monitoring each phase of my deteriorating condition. My acceptance of the illness followed several months of denial during which, at first, I had ascribed the malaise and restlessness and sudden fits of anxiety to withdrawal from alcohol; I had abruptly abandoned whiskey and all other intoxicants that June.

During the course of my worsening emotional climate I had read a certain amount on the subject of depression, both in books tailored for the layman and in weightier professional works including the psychiatrists' bible, *DSM* (*The Diagnostic and Statistical Manual of the American Psychiatric Association*). Throughout much of my life I have been compelled, perhaps unwisely, to become an autodidact in medicine, and have accumulated a better-than-average amateur's knowledge about medical matters (to which many of my friends, surely unwisely, have often deferred), and so it came as an astonishment to me that I was close to a total ignoramus about depression, which can be as serious a medical affair as diabetes or cancer. Most likely, as an incipient depressive, I had always subconsciously rejected or ignored the proper knowledge; it cut too close to the psychic bone, and I shoved it aside as an unwelcome addition to my store of information.

At any rate, during the few hours when the depressive state itself eased off long enough to permit the luxury of concentration, I had recently filled this vacuum with fairly extensive reading and I had absorbed many fascinating and troubling facts, which, however, I could not put to practical use. The most honest authorities face up square to the fact that serious de-

9

pression is not readily treatable. Unlike, let us say, diabetes, where immediate measures taken to rearrange the body's adaptation to glucose can dramatically reverse a dangerous process and bring it under control, depression in its major stages possesses no quickly available remedy: failure of alleviation is one of the most distressing factors of the disorder as it reveals itself to the victim, and one that helps situate it squarely in the category of grave diseases. Except in those maladies strictly designated as malignant or degenerative, we expect *some* kind of treatment and eventual amelioration, by pills or physical therapy or diet or surgery, with a logical progression from the initial relief of symptoms to final cure. Frighteningly, the layman-sufferer from major depression, taking a peek into some of the many books currently on the market, will find much in the way of theory and symptomatology and very little that legitimately suggests the possibility of quick rescue. Those that do claim an easy way out are glib and most likely fraudulent. There are decent popular works which intelligently point the way toward treatment and cure, demonstrating how certain therapies—psychotherapy or pharmacology, or a combination of these—can indeed restore people to health in all but the most persistent and devastating cases; but the wisest books among them underscore the hard truth that serious depressions do not disappear overnight. All of this emphasizes an essential though difficult reality which I think needs stating at the outset of my own chronicle: the disease of depression remains a great mystery. It has yielded its secrets to science far more reluctantly than many of the other major ills besetting us. The intense and sometimes comically strident factionalism that exists in present-day psychiatry—the schism between the believers in psychotherapy and the adherents of pharmacology—resembles the medical quarrels of the eighteenth century (to bleed or not to bleed) and almost defines in itself the inexplicable nature of depression and the difficulty of its treatment. As a clinician in the field told me honestly and, I think, with a striking deftness of analogy: "If you compare our knowledge with Columbus's discovery of America, America is yet unknown; we are still down on that little island in the Bahamas."

In my reading I had learned, for example, that in at least one interesting respect my own case was atypical. Most people who begin to suffer from the illness are laid low in the morning, with such malefic effect that they are unable to get out of bed. They feel better only as the day wears on. But my situation was just the reverse. While I was able to rise and function almost normally during the earlier part of the day, I began to sense the onset of the symptoms at midafternoon or a little later—gloom crowding in on me, a sense of dread and alienation and, above all, stifling anxiety. I suspect that it is basically a matter of indifference whether one suffers the most in the morning or the evening: if these states of excruciating near-paralysis are similar, as they probably are, the question of timing would seem to be academic. But it was no doubt the turnabout of the usual daily onset of symptoms that allowed me that morning in Paris to proceed without mishap, feeling more or less self-possessed, to the gloriously ornate palace on the Right Bank that houses the Fondation Cino del Duca. There, in a rococo salon, I was presented with the award before a small crowd of French cultural figures, and made my speech of acceptance with what I felt was passable aplomb, stating that while I was donating the bulk of my prize money to various organizations fostering French-American goodwill, including the American Hospital in Neuilly, there was a limit to altruism (this spoken jokingly) and so I hoped it would not be taken amiss if I held back a small portion for myself.

What I did not say, and which was no joke, was that

the amount I was withholding was to pay for two tickets the next day on the Concorde, so that I might return speedily with Rose to the United States, where just a few days before I had made an appointment to see a psychiatrist. For reasons that I'm sure had to do with a reluctance to accept the reality that my mind was dissolving, I had avoided seeking psychiatric aid during the past weeks, as my distress intensified. But I knew I couldn't delay the confrontation indefinitely, and when I did finally make contact by telephone with a highly recommended therapist, he encouraged me to make the Paris trip, telling me that he would see me as soon as I returned. I very much needed to get back, and fast. Despite the evidence that I was in serious difficulty, I wanted to maintain the rosy view. A lot of the literature available concerning depression is, as I say, breezily optimistic, spreading assurances that nearly all depressive states will be stabilized or reversed if only the suitable antidepressant can be found; the reader is of course easily swayed by promises of quick remedy. In Paris, even as I delivered my remarks, I had a need for the day to be over, felt a consuming urgency to fly to America and the office of the doctor, who would whisk my malaise away with his miraculous medications. I recollect that moment clearly now, and am hardly able to believe that I possessed such ingenuous hope, or that I could have been so unaware of the trouble and peril that lay ahead.

Simone del Duca, a large dark-haired woman of queenly manner, was understandably incredulous at first, and then enraged, when after the presentation ceremony I told her that I could not join her at lunch upstairs in the great mansion, along with a dozen or so members of the Académie Française, who had chosen me for the prize. My refusal was both emphatic and simpleminded; I told her point-blank that I had arranged instead to have lunch at a restaurant with my French publisher, Françoise Gallimard. Of course this decision on my part was outrageous; it had been announced months before to me and everyone else concerned that a luncheon—moreover, a luncheon in my honor—was part of the day's pageantry. But my behavior was really the result of the illness, which had progressed far enough to produce some of its most famous and sinister hallmarks: confusion, failure of mental focus and lapse of memory. At a later stage my entire mind would be dominated by anarchic disconnections; as I have said, there was now something that resembled bifurcation of mood: lucidity of sorts in the early hours of the day, gathering murk in the afternoon and evening. It must have been during the previous evening's murky distractedness that I made the luncheon date with Françoise Gallimard, forgetting my del Duca obligations. That decision continued to completely master my thinking, creating in me such obstinate determination that now I was able to blandly insult the worthy Simone del Duca. *"Alors!"* she exclaimed to me, and her face flushed angrily as she whirled in a stately volte-face, *"au . . . re-voir!"* Suddenly I was flabbergasted, stunned with horror at what I had done. I fantasized a table at which sat the hostess and the Académie Française, the guest of honor at La Coupole. I implored Madame's assistant, a bespectacled woman with a clipboard and an ashen, mortified expression, to try to reinstate me: it was all a terrible mistake, a mixup, a *malentendu*. And then I blurted some words that a lifetime of general equilibrium, and a smug belief in the impregnability of my psychic health, had prevented me from believing I could ever utter; I was chilled as I heard myself speak them to this perfect stranger. "I'm sick," I said, *"un problème psychiatrique."*

Madame del Duca was magnanimous in accepting my apology and the lunch went off without further strain, although I couldn't completely rid myself of the suspicion, as we chatted somewhat stiffly, that my benefactress was still disturbed by my conduct and thought me a weird number. The lunch was a long one, and when it was over I felt myself entering the afternoon shadows with their encroaching anxiety and dread. A television crew from one of the national channels was waiting (I had forgotten about them, too), ready to take me to the newly opened Picasso Museum, where I was supposed to be filmed looking at the exhibits and exchanging comments with Rose. This turned out to be, as I knew it would, not a captivating promenade but a demanding struggle, a major ordeal. By the time we arrived at the museum, having dealt with heavy traffic, it was past four o'clock and my brain had begun to endure its familiar siege: panic and dislocation, and a sense that my thought processes were being engulfed by a toxic and unnameable tide that obliterated any enjoyable response to the living world. This is to say more specifically that instead of pleasure—certainly instead of the pleasure I should be having in this sumptuous showcase of bright genius— I was feeling in my mind a sensation close to, but indescribably different from, actual pain. This leads me to touch again on the elusive nature of such distress. That the word "indescribable" should present itself is not fortuitous, since it has to be emphasized that if the pain were readily describable most of the countless sufferers from this ancient affliction would have been able to confidently depict for their friends and loved ones (even their physicians) some of the actual dimensions of their torment, and perhaps elicit a comprehension that has been generally lacking; such incomprehension has usually been due not to a failure of sympathy but to the basic inability of healthy people to imagine a form of torment so alien to everyday experience. For myself, the pain is most closely connected to drowning or suffocation—but even these images are off the mark. William James, who battled depression for many years, gave up the search for an adequate portrayal, implying its near-impossibility when he wrote in *The Varieties of Religious Experience:* "It is a positive and active anguish, a sort of psychical neuralgia wholly unknown to normal life."

The pain persisted during my museum tour and reached a crescendo in the next few hours when, back at the hotel, I fell onto the bed and lay gazing at the ceiling, nearly immobilized and in a trance of supreme discomfort. Rational thought was usually absent from my mind at such times, hence *trance*. I can think of no more apposite word for this state of being, a condition of helpless stupor in which cognition was replaced by that "positive and active anguish." And one of the most unendurable aspects of such an interlude was the inability to sleep. It had been my custom of a near-lifetime, like that of vast numbers of people, to settle myself into a soothing nap in the late afternoon, but the disruption of normal sleep patterns is a notoriously devastating feature of depression; to the injurious sleeplessness with which I had been afflicted each night was added the insult of this afternoon insomnia, diminutive by comparison but all the more horrendous because it struck during the hours of the most intense misery. It had become clear that I would never be granted even a few minutes' relief from my full-time exhaustion. I clearly recall thinking, as I lay there while Rose sat nearby reading, that my afternoons and evenings were becoming almost measurably worse, and that this episode was the worst to date. But I somehow managed to reassemble myself for dinner with—who else?—Françoise Gallimard, co-victim along with Simone del Duca of the frightful lunchtime contretemps. The night was blustery and raw, with a chill wet wind blowing down the avenues, and when Rose and I met Françoise and her son and a friend at La Lorraine, a glittering brasserie not far from L'Étoile, rain was descending from the heavens in torrents. Someone in the group, sensing my state of mind, apologized for the evil night, but I recall thinking that even if this were one of those warmly scented and passionate evenings for which Paris is celebrated I would respond like the zombie I had become. The weather of depression is unmodulated, its light a brownout.

And zombielike, halfway through the dinner, I lost the del Duca prize check for $25,000. Having tucked the check in the inside breast pocket of my jacket, I let my hand stray idly to that place and realized that it was gone. Did I "intend" to lose the money? Recently I had been deeply bothered that I was not deserving of the prize. I believe in the reality of the accidents we subconsciously perpetrate on ourselves, and so how easy it was for this loss to be not loss but a form of repudiation, offshoot of that self-loathing (depression's premier badge) by which I was persuaded that I could not be worthy of the prize, that I was in fact not worthy of any of the recognition that had come my way in the past few years. Whatever the reason for its disappearance, the check was gone, and its loss dovetailed well with the other failures of the dinner: my failure to have an appetite for the grand *plateau de fruits de mer* placed before me, failure of even forced laughter and, at last, virtually total failure of speech. At this point the ferocious *inwardness* of the pain produced an immense distraction that prevented my articulating words beyond a hoarse murmur; I sensed myself turning wall-eyed, monosyllabic, and also I sensed my French friends becoming uneasily aware of my predicament. It was a scene from a bad operetta by now: all of us near the floor, searching for the vanished money. Just as I signaled that it was time to go, Françoise's son discovered the check, which had somehow slipped out of my pocket and fluttered under an adjoining table, and we went forth into the rainy night. Then, while I was riding in the car, I thought of Albert Camus and Romain Gary.

I I

WHEN I WAS A YOUNG WRITER THERE HAD BEEN A stage where Camus, almost more than any other contemporary literary figure, radically set the tone for my own view of life and history. I read his novel *The Stranger* somewhat later than I should have—I was in my early thirties—but after finishing it I received the stab of recognition that proceeds from reading the work of a writer who has wedded moral passion to a style of great beauty and whose unblinking vision is capable of frightening the soul to its marrow. The cosmic loneliness of Meursault, the hero of that novel, so haunted me that when I set out to write *The Confessions of Nat Turner* I was impelled to use Camus's device of having the story flow from the point of view of a narrator isolated in his jail cell during the hours before his execution. For me there was a spiritual connection between Meursault's frigid solitude and the plight of Nat Turner—his rebel predecessor in history by a hundred years—likewise condemned and abandoned by man and God. Camus's essay "Reflections on the Guillotine" is a virtually unique document, freighted with terrible and fiery logic; it is difficult to conceive of the most vengeful supporter of the death penalty retaining the same attitude after exposure to scathing truths expressed with such ardor and precision. I know my thinking was forever altered by that work, not only turning me around completely, convincing me of the essential barbarism of capital punishment, but establishing substantial claims on my conscience in regard to matters of responsibility at large. Camus was a great cleanser of my intellect, ridding me of countless sluggish ideas, and through some of the most unsettling pessimism I had ever encountered causing me to be aroused anew by life's enigmatic promise.

The disappointment I always felt at never meeting Camus was compounded by that failure having been such a near miss. I had planned to see him in 1960, when I was traveling to France and had been told in a letter by the writer Romain Gary that he was going to arrange a dinner in Paris where I would meet Camus. The enormously gifted Gary, whom I knew slightly at the time and who later became a cherished friend, had informed me that Camus, whom he saw frequently, had read my *Un Lit de Ténèbres* and had admired it; I was of course greatly flattered and felt that a get-together would be a splendid happening. But before I arrived in France there came the appalling news: Camus had been in an automobile crash, and was dead at the cruelly young age of forty-six. I have almost never felt so intensely the loss of someone I didn't know. I pondered his death endlessly. Although Camus had not been driving he supposedly knew the driver, who was the son of his publisher, to be a speed demon; so there was an element of recklessness in the accident that bore overtones of the near-suicidal, at least of a death flirtation, and it was inevitable that conjectures concerning the event should revert back to the theme of suicide in the writer's work. One of the century's most famous intellectual pronouncements comes at the beginning of *The Myth of Sisyphus:* "There is but one truly serious philosophical problem, and that is suicide. Judging whether life is or is not worth living amounts to answering the fundamental question of philosophy." Reading this for the first time I was puzzled and continued to be throughout much of the essay, since despite the work's persuasive logic and eloquence there was a lot that eluded me, and I always came back to grapple vainly with the initial hypothesis, unable to deal with the premise that anyone should come close to wishing to kill himself in the first place. A later short novel, *The Fall,* I admired with reservations; the guilt and self-condemnation of the lawyer-narrator, gloomily spinning out his monologue in an Amsterdam bar, seemed a touch clamorous and excessive, but at the time of my reading I was unable to perceive that the lawyer was behaving very much like a man in the throes of clinical depression. Such was my innocence of the very existence of this disease.

Camus, Romain told me, occasionally hinted at his own deep despondency and had spoken of suicide. Sometimes he spoke in jest, but the jest had the quality of sour wine, upsetting Romain. Yet apparently he made no attempts and so perhaps it was not coincidental that, despite its abiding tone of melancholy, a sense of the triumph of life over death is at the core of *The Myth of Sisyphus* with its austere message: in the absence of hope we must still struggle to survive, and so we do—by the skin of our teeth. It was only after the passing of some years that it seemed credible to me that Camus's statement about suicide, and his general preoccupation with the subject, might have sprung at least as strongly from some persistent disturbance of mood as from his concerns with ethics and epistemology. Gary again discussed at length his assumptions about Camus's depression during August of 1978, when I had lent him my guest cottage in Connecticut, and I came down from my summer home on Martha's Vineyard to pay him a weekend visit. As we talked I felt that some of Romain's suppositions about the seriousness of Camus's recurring despair gained weight from the fact that he, too, had begun to suffer from depression, and he freely admitted as much. It was not incapacitating, he insisted, and he had it under control, but he felt it from time to time, this leaden and poisonous mood the color of verdigris, so incongruous in the midst of the lush New England summer. A

Russian Jew born in Lithuania, Romain had always seemed possessed of an Eastern European melancholy, so it was hard to tell the difference. Nonetheless, he was hurting. He said that he was able to perceive a flicker of the desperate state of mind which had been described to him by Camus.

Gary's situation was hardly lightened by the presence of Jean Seberg, his Iowa-born actress wife, from whom he had been divorced and, I thought, long estranged. I learned that she was there because their son, Diego, was at a nearby tennis camp. Their presumed estrangement made me surprised to see her living with Romain, surprised too—no, shocked and saddened—by her appearance: all her once fragile and luminous blond beauty had disappeared into a puffy mask. She moved like a sleepwalker, said little, and had the blank gaze of someone tranquilized (or drugged, or both) nearly to the point of catalepsy. I understood how devoted they still were, and was touched by his solicitude, both tender and paternal. Romain told me that Jean was being treated for the disorder that afflicted him, and mentioned something about antidepressant medications, but none of this registered very strongly, and also meant little. This memory of my relative indifference is important because such indifference demonstrates powerfully the outsider's inability to grasp the essence of the illness. Camus's depression and now Romain Gary's—and certainly Jean's—were abstract ailments to me, in spite of my sympathy, and I hadn't an inkling of its true contours or the nature of the pain so many victims experience as the mind continues in its insidious meltdown.

In Paris that October night I knew that I, too, was in the process of meltdown. And on the way to the hotel in the car I had a clear revelation. A disruption of the circadian cycle—the metabolic and glandular rhythms that are central to our workaday life—seems to be involved in many, if not most, cases of depression; this is why brutal insomnia so often occurs and is most likely why each day's pattern of distress exhibits fairly predictable alternating periods of intensity and relief. The evening's relief for me—an incomplete but noticeable letup, like the change from a torrential downpour to a steady shower—came in the hours after dinnertime and before midnight, when the pain lifted a little and my mind would become lucid enough to focus on matters beyond the immediate upheaval convulsing my system. Naturally I looked forward to this period, for sometimes I felt close to being reasonably sane, and that night in the car I was aware of a semblance of clarity returning, along with the ability to think rational thoughts. Having been able to reminisce about Camus and Romain Gary, however, I found that my continuing thoughts were not very consoling.

The memory of Jean Seberg gripped me with sadness. A little over a year after our encounter in Connecticut she took an overdose of pills and was found dead in a car parked in a cul-de-sac off a Paris avenue, where her body had lain for many days. The following year I sat with Romain at the Brasserie Lipp during a long lunch while he told me that, despite their difficulties, his loss of Jean had so deepened his depression that from time to time he had been rendered nearly helpless. But even then I was unable to comprehend the nature of his anguish. I remembered that his hands trembled and, though he could hardly be called superannuated—he was in his mid-sixties—his voice had the wheezy sound of very old age that I now realized was, or could be, the voice of depression; in the vortex of my severest pain I had begun to develop that ancient voice myself. I never saw Romain again. Claude Gallimard, Françoise's father, had recollected to me how, in 1980, only a few hours after another lunch where the talk between the two old friends had been composed and casual, even lighthearted, certainly anything but somber, Romain Gary—twice winner of the Prix Goncourt (one of these awards pseudonymous, the result of his having gleefully tricked the critics), hero of the Republic, valorous recipient of the Croix de Guerre, diplomat, bon vivant, womanizer par excellence—went home to his apartment on the rue du Bac and put a bullet through his brain.

It was at some point during the course of these musings that the sign HÔTEL WASHINGTON swam across my vision, bringing back memories of my long-ago arrival in the city, along with the fierce and sudden realization that I would never see Paris again. This certitude astonished me and filled me with a new fright, for while thoughts of death had long been common during my siege, blowing through my mind like icy gusts of wind, they were the formless shapes of doom that I suppose are dreamed of by people in the grip of any severe affliction. The difference now was in the sure understanding that tomorrow, when the pain descended once more, or the tomorrow after that—certainly on some not-too-distant tomorrow—I would be forced to judge that life was not worth living and thereby answer, for myself at least, the fundamental question of philosophy.

III

To many of us who knew Abbie Hoffman even slightly, as I did, his death in the spring of 1989 was a sorrowful happening. Just past the age of fifty, he had been too young and apparently too vital for such an ending; a feeling of chagrin and dreadfulness attends the news of nearly anyone's suicide, and Abbie's death seemed to me especially cruel. I had first met him during the wild days and nights of the 1968 Democratic Convention in Chicago, where I had gone to write a piece for *The New York Review of Books,* and I later was one of those who testified in behalf of him and his fellow defendants at the trial, also in Chicago, in 1970. Amid the pious follies and morbid perversions of American life, his antic style was exhilarating, and it was hard not to admire the hell-raising and the brio, the anarchic individualism. I wish I had seen more of him in recent years; his sudden death left me with a particular emptiness, as suicides usually do to everyone. But the event was given a further dimension of poignancy by what one must begin to regard as a predictable reaction from many: the denial, the refusal to accept the fact of the suicide itself, as if the voluntary act—as opposed to an accident, or death from natural causes—were tinged with a delinquency that somehow lessened the man and his character.

Abbie's brother appeared on television, grief-ravaged and distraught; one could not help feeling compassion as he sought to deflect the idea of suicide, insisting that Abbie, after all, had always been careless with pills and would never have left his family bereft. However, the coroner confirmed that Hoffman had taken the equivalent of 150 phenobarbitals. It's quite natural that the people closest to suicide victims so frequently and feverishly hasten to disclaim the truth; the sense of implication, of personal guilt—the idea that one might have prevented the act if one had taken certain precautions, had somehow behaved differently—is perhaps inevitable. Even so, the sufferer—whether he has actually killed himself or attempted to do so, or merely expressed threats—is often, through denial on the part of others, unjustly made to appear a wrongdoer.

A similar case is that of Randall Jarrell—one of the fine poets and critics of his generation—who on a night in 1965, near Chapel Hill, North Carolina, was struck by a car and killed. Jarrell's presence on that particular stretch of road, at an odd hour of the evening, was puzzling, and since some of the indications were that he had deliberately let the car strike him, the early conclusion was that his death was suicide. *Newsweek,* among other publications, said as much, but Jarrell's widow protested in a letter to that magazine; there was a hue and cry from many of his friends and supporters, and a coroner's jury eventually ruled the death to be accidental. Jarrell had been suffering from extreme depression and had been hospitalized; only a few months before his misadventure on the highway and while in the hospital, he had slashed his wrists.

Anyone who is acquainted with some of the jagged contours of Jarrell's life—including his violent fluctuations of mood, his fits of black despondency—and who, in addition, has acquired a basic knowledge of the danger signals of depression, would seriously question the verdict of the coroner's jury. But the stigma of self-inflicted death is for some people a hateful blot that demands erasure at all costs. (More than two decades after his death, in the Summer 1986 issue of *The American Scholar,* a one time student of Jarrell's, reviewing a collection of the poet's letters, made the review less a literary or biographical appraisal than an occasion for continuing to try to exorcise the vile phantom of suicide.)

Randall Jarrell almost certainly killed himself. He did so not because he was a coward, nor out of any moral feebleness, but because he was afflicted with a depression that was so devastating that he could no longer endure the pain of it.

This general unawareness of what depression is really like was apparent most recently in the matter of Primo Levi, the remarkable Italian writer and survivor of Auschwitz who, at the age of sixty-seven, hurled himself down a stairwell in Turin in 1987. Since my own involvement with the illness, I had been more than ordinarily interested in Levi's death, and so, late in 1988, when I read an account in *The New York Times* about a symposium on the writer and his work held at New York University, I was fascinated but, finally, appalled. For, according to the article, many of the participants, worldly writers and scholars, seemed mystified by Levi's suicide, mystified and disappointed. It was as if this man whom they had all so greatly admired, and who had endured so much at the hands of the Nazis—a man of exemplary resilience and courage—had by his suicide demonstrated a frailty, a crumbling of character they were loath to accept. In the face of a terrible absolute—self-destruction—their reaction was helplessness and (the reader could not avoid it) a touch of shame.

My annoyance over all this was so intense that I was prompted to write a short piece for the op-ed page of the *Times*. The argument I put forth was fairly straightforward: the pain of severe depression is quite unimaginable to those who have not suffered it, and it kills in many instances because its anguish can no longer be borne. The prevention of many suicides will continue to be hindered until there is a general awareness of the nature of this pain. Through the healing process of time—and through medical intervention or hospitalization in many cases—most people survive depression, which may be its only blessing; but to the tragic legion who are compelled to destroy themselves there should be no more reproof attached than to the victims of terminal cancer.

I had set down my thoughts in this *Times* piece rather hurriedly and spontaneously, but the response was equally spontaneous—and enormous. It had taken, I speculated, no particular originality or boldness on my part to speak out frankly about suicide and the impulse toward it, but I had apparently underestimated the number of people for whom the subject had been taboo, a matter of secrecy and shame. The overwhelming reaction made me feel that inadvertently I had helped unlock a closet from which many souls were eager to come out and proclaim that they, too, had experienced the feelings I had described. It is the only time in my life I have felt it worthwhile to have invaded my own privacy, and to make that privacy public. And I thought that, given such momentum, and with my experience in Paris as a detailed example of what occurs during depression, it would be useful to try to chronicle some of my own experiences with the illness and in the process perhaps establish a frame of reference out of which one or more valuable conclusions might be drawn. Such conclusions, it has to be emphasized, must still be based on the events that happened to one man. In setting these reflections down I don't intend my ordeal to stand as a representation of what happens, or might happen, to others. Depression is much too complex in its cause, its symptoms and its treatment for unqualified conclusions to be drawn from the experience of a single individual. Although as an illness depression manifests certain unvarying characteristics, it also allows for many idiosyncrasies; I've been amazed at some of the freakish phenomena—not reported by other patients—that it has wrought amid the twistings of my mind's labyrinth.

Depression afflicts millions directly, and millions more who are relatives or friends of victims. It has been estimated that as many as one in ten Americans will suffer from the illness. As assertively democratic as a Norman Rockwell poster, it strikes indiscriminately at all ages, races, creeds and classes, though women are at considerably higher risk than men. The occupational list (dressmakers, barge captains, sushi chefs, cabinet members) of its patients is too long and tedious to give here; it is enough to say that very few people escape being a potential victim of the disease, at least in its milder form. Despite depression's eclectic reach, it has been demonstrated with fair convincingness that artistic types (especially poets) are particularly vulnerable to the disorder—which, in its graver, clinical manifestation takes upward of twenty percent of its victims by way of suicide. Just a few of these fallen artists, all modern, make up a sad but scintillant roll call: Hart Crane, Vincent van Gogh, Virginia Woolf, Arshile Gorky, Cesare Pavese, Romain Gary, Vachel Lindsay, Sylvia Plath, Henry de Montherlant, Mark Rothko, John Berryman, Jack London, Ernest Hemingway, William Inge, Diane Arbus, Tadeusz Borowski, Paul

Celan, Anne Sexton, Sergei Esenin, Vladimir Maya-kovsky—the list goes on. (The Russian poet Maya-kovsky was harshly critical of his great contemporary Esenin's suicide a few years before, which should stand as a caveat for all who are judgmental about self-destruction.) When one thinks of these doomed and splendidly creative men and women, one is drawn to contemplate their childhoods, where, to the best of anyone's knowledge, the seeds of the illness take strong root; could any of them have had a hint, then, of the psyche's perishability, its exquisite fragility? And why were they destroyed, while others—similarly stricken —struggled through?

I V

WHEN I WAS FIRST AWARE THAT I HAD BEEN LAID low by the disease, I felt a need, among other things, to register a strong protest against the word "depression." Depression, most people know, used to be termed "melancholia," a word which appears in English as early as the year 1303 and crops up more than once in Chaucer, who in his usage seemed to be aware of its pathological nuances. "Melancholia" would still appear to be a far more apt and evocative word for the blacker forms of the disorder, but it was usurped by a noun with a bland tonality and lacking any magisterial presence, used indifferently to describe an economic decline or a rut in the ground, a true wimp of a word for such a major illness. It may be that the scientist generally held responsible for its currency in modern times, a Johns Hopkins Medical School faculty member justly venerated—the Swiss-born psychiatrist Adolf Meyer—had a tin ear for the finer rhythms of English and therefore was unaware of the semantic damage he had inflicted by offering "depression" as a descriptive noun for such a dreadful and raging disease. Nonetheless, for over seventy-five years the word has slithered innocuously through the language like a slug, leaving little trace of its intrinsic malevolence and preventing, by its very insipidity, a general awareness of the horrible intensity of the disease when out of control.

As one who has suffered from the malady in extremis yet returned to tell the tale, I would lobby for a truly arresting designation. "Brainstorm," for instance, has unfortunately been preempted to describe, somewhat jocularly, intellectual inspiration. But something along these lines is needed. Told that someone's mood disorder has evolved into a storm—a veritable howling tempest in the brain, which is indeed what a clinical depression resembles like nothing else—even the uninformed layman might display sympathy rather than the standard reaction that "depression" evokes, something akin to "So what?" or "You'll pull out of it" or "We all have bad days." The phrase "nervous breakdown" seems to be on its way out, certainly deservedly so, owing to its insinuation of a vague spinelessness, but we still seem destined to be saddled with "depression" until a better, sturdier name is created.

The depression that engulfed me was not of the manic type—the one accompanied by euphoric highs—which would have most probably presented itself earlier in my life. I was sixty when the illness struck for the first time, in the "unipolar" form, which leads straight down. I shall never learn what "caused" my depression, as no one will ever learn about their own. To be able to do so will likely forever prove to be an impossibility, so complex are the intermingled factors of abnormal chemistry, behavior and genetics. Plainly, multiple components are involved—perhaps three or four, most probably more, in fathomless permutations. That is why the greatest fallacy about suicide lies in the belief that there is a single immediate answer—or perhaps combined answers—as to why the deed was done.

The inevitable question "Why did he [or she] do it?" usually leads to odd speculations, for the most part fallacies themselves. Reasons were quickly advanced for Abbie Hoffman's death: his reaction to an auto accident he had suffered, the failure of his most recent book, his mother's serious illness. With Randall Jarrell it was a declining career cruelly epitomized by a vicious book review and his consequent anguish. Primo Levi, it was rumored, had been burdened by caring for his paralytic mother, which was more onerous to his spirit than even his experience at Auschwitz. Any one of these factors may have lodged like a thorn in the sides of the three men, and been a torment. Such aggravations may be crucial and cannot be ignored. But most people quietly endure the equivalent of injuries, declining careers, nasty book reviews, family illnesses. A vast majority of the survivors of Auschwitz have borne up fairly well. Bloody and bowed by the outrages of life, most human beings still stagger on down the road, unscathed by real depression. To discover why some people plunge into the downward spiral of depression, one must search beyond the manifest crisis—and then still fail to come up with anything beyond wise conjecture.

The storm which swept me into a hospital in December began as a cloud no bigger than a wine goblet the previous June. And the cloud—the manifest crisis—involved alcohol, a substance I had been abusing for forty years. Like a great many American writers, whose sometimes lethal addiction to alcohol has become so legendary as to provide in itself a stream of studies and books, I used alcohol as the magical conduit to fantasy and euphoria, and to the enhancement of the imagination. There is no need to either rue or apologize for my use of this soothing, often sublime agent, which had contributed greatly to my writing; although I never set down a line while under its influence, I did use it—often in conjunction with music—as a means to let my mind conceive visions that the unaltered, sober brain has no access to. Alcohol was an invaluable senior partner of my intellect, besides being a friend whose ministrations I sought daily—sought also, I now see, as a means to calm the anxiety and incipient dread that I had hidden away for so long somewhere in the dungeons of my spirit.

The trouble was, at the beginning of this particular

summer, that I was betrayed. It struck me quite suddenly, almost overnight: I could no longer drink. It was as if my body had risen up in protest, along with my mind, and had conspired to reject this daily mood bath which it had so long welcomed and, who knows? perhaps even come to need. Many drinkers have experienced this intolerance as they have grown older. I suspect that the crisis was at least partly metabolic—the liver rebelling, as if to say, "No more, no more"—but at any rate I discovered that alcohol in minuscule amounts, even a mouthful of wine, caused me nausea, a desperate and unpleasant wooziness, a sinking sensation and ultimately a distinct revulsion. The comforting friend had abandoned me not gradually and reluctantly, as a true friend might do, but like a shot—and I was left high and certainly dry, and unhelmed.

Neither by will nor by choice had I became an abstainer; the situation was puzzling to me, but it was also traumatic, and I date the onset of my depressive mood from the beginning of this deprivation. Logically, one would be overjoyed that the body had so summarily dismissed a substance that was undermining its health; it was as if my system had generated a form of Antabuse, which should have allowed me to happily go my way, satisfied that a trick of nature had shut me off from a harmful dependence. But, instead, I began to experience a vaguely troubling malaise, a sense of something having gone cockeyed in the domestic universe I'd dwelt in so long, so comfortably. While depression is by no means unknown when people stop drinking, it is usually on a scale that is not menacing. But it should be kept in mind how idiosyncratic the faces of depression can be.

It was not really alarming at first, since the change was subtle, but I did notice that my surroundings took on a different tone at certain times: the shadows of nightfall seemed more somber, my mornings were less buoyant, walks in the woods became less zestful, and there was a moment during my working hours in the late afternoon when a kind of panic and anxiety overtook me, just for a few minutes, accompanied by a visceral queasiness—such a seizure was at least slightly alarming, after all. As I set down these recollections, I realize that it should have been plain to me that I was already in the grip of the beginning of a mood disorder, but I was ignorant of such a condition at that time.

When I reflected on this curious alteration of my consciousness—and I was baffled enough from time to time to do so—I assumed that it all had to do somehow with my enforced withdrawal from alcohol. And, of course, to a certain extent this was true. But it is my conviction now that alcohol played a perverse trick on me when we said farewell to each other: although, as everyone should know, it is a major depressant, it had never truly depressed me during my drinking career, acting instead as a shield against anxiety. Suddenly vanished, the great ally which for so long had kept my demons at bay was no longer there to prevent those demons from beginning to swarm through the subconscious, and I was emotionally naked, vulnerable as I had never been before. Doubtless depression had hovered near me for years, waiting to swoop down. Now I was in the first stage—premonitory, like a flicker of sheet lightning barely perceived—of depression's black tempest.

I was on Martha's Vineyard, where I've spent a good part of each year since the 1960s, during that exceptionally beautiful summer. But I had begun to respond indifferently to the island's pleasures. I felt a kind of numbness, an enervation, but more particularly an odd fragility—as if my body had actually become frail, hypersensitive and somehow disjointed and clumsy, lacking normal coordination. And soon I was in the throes of a pervasive hypochondria. Nothing felt quite right with my corporeal self; there were twitches and pains, sometimes intermittent, often seemingly constant, that seemed to presage all sorts of dire infirmities. (Given these signs, one can understand how, as far back as the seventeenth century—in the notes of contemporary physicians, and in the perceptions of John Dryden and others—a connection is made between melancholia and hypochondria; the words are often interchangeable, and were so used until the nineteenth century by writers as various as Sir Walter Scott and the Brontës, who also linked melancholy to a preoccupation with bodily ills.) It is easy to see how this condition is part of the psyche's apparatus of defense: unwilling to accept its own gathering deterioration, the mind announces to its indwelling consciousness that it is the body with its perhaps correctable defects—not the precious and irreplaceable mind—that is going haywire.

In my case, the overall effect was immensely disturbing, augmenting the anxiety that was by now never quite absent from my waking hours and fueling still another strange behavior pattern—a fidgety recklessness that kept me on the move, somewhat to the perplexity of my family and friends. Once, in late summer, on an airplane trip to New York, I made the reckless mistake of downing a scotch and soda—my first alcohol in months—which promptly sent me into a tailspin, causing me such a horrified sense of disease and interior doom that the very next day I rushed to a Manhattan internist, who inaugurated a long series of tests. Normally I would have been satisfied, indeed elated, when, after three weeks of high-tech and extremely expensive evaluation, the doctor pronounced me totally fit; and I *was* happy, for a day or two, until there once again began the rhythmic daily erosion of my mood—anxiety, agitation, unfocused dread.

By now I had moved back to my house in Connecticut. It was October, and one of the unforgettable features of this stage of my disorder was the way in which my own farmhouse, my beloved home for thirty years, took on for me at that point when my spirits regularly sank to their nadir an almost palpable quality of ominousness. The fading evening light—akin to that famous "slant of light" of Emily Dickinson's, which spoke to her of death, of chill extinction—had none of its familiar autumnal loveliness, but ensnared me in a suffocating gloom. I wondered how this friendly place, teeming with such memories of (again in her words) "Lads and Girls," of "laughter and ability and Sighing, / And Frocks and Curls," could almost perceptibly seem so hostile and forbidding. Physically, I was not alone. As always Rose was present and listened with unflagging patience to my complaints. But I felt an immense and aching solitude. I could no longer concentrate during those afternoon hours, which for years had been my working time, and the act of writing itself, becoming more and more difficult and exhausting, stalled, then finally ceased.

There were also dreadful, pouncing seizures of anxiety. One bright day on a walk through the woods with my dog I heard a flock of Canada geese honking high above trees ablaze with foliage; ordinarily a sight and sound that would have exhilarated me, the flight of birds caused me to stop, riveted with fear, and I stood stranded there, helpless, shivering, aware for the first time that I had been stricken by no mere pangs of withdrawal but by a serious illness whose name and actuality I was able finally to acknowledge. Going home, I couldn't rid my mind of the line of Baudelaire's, dredged up from the distant past, that for several days had been skittering around at the edge of my consciousness: "I have felt the wind of the wing of madness."

Our perhaps understandable modern need to dull the sawtooth edges of so many of the afflictions we are heir to has led us to banish the harsh old-fashioned words: madhouse, asylum, insanity, melancholia, lunatic, madness. But never let it be doubted that depression, in its extreme form, is madness. The madness results from an aberrant biochemical process. It has been established with reasonable certainty (after strong resistance from many psychiatrists, and not all that long ago) that such madness is chemically induced amid the neurotransmitters of the brain, probably as the result of systemic stress, which for unknown reasons causes a depletion of the chemicals norepinephrine and serotonin, and the increase of a hormone, cortisol. With all of this upheaval in the brain tissues, the alternate drenching and deprivation, it is no wonder that the mind begins to feel aggrieved, stricken, and the muddied thought processes register the distress of an organ in convulsion. Sometimes, though not very often, such a disturbed mind will turn to violent thoughts regarding others. But with their minds turned agonizingly inward, people with depression are usually dangerous only to themselves. The madness of depression is, generally speaking, the antithesis of violence. It is a storm indeed, but a storm of murk. Soon evident are the slowed-down responses, near paralysis, psychic energy throttled back close to zero. Ultimately, the body is affected and feels sapped, drained.

That fall, as the disorder gradually took full possession of my system, I began to conceive that my mind itself was like one of those outmoded small-town telephone exchanges, being gradually inundated by floodwaters: one by one, the normal circuits began to drown, causing some of the functions of the body and nearly all of those of instinct and intellect to slowly disconnect.

There is a well-known checklist of some of these functions and their failures. Mine conked out fairly close to schedule, many of them following the pattern of depressive seizures. I particularly remember the lamentable near disappearance of my voice. It underwent a strange transformation, becoming at times quite faint, wheezy and spasmodic—a friend observed later that it was the voice of a ninety-year-old. The libido also made an early exit, as it does in most major illnesses—it is the superfluous need of a body in beleaguered emergency. Many people lose all appetite; mine was relatively normal, but I found myself eating only for subsistence: food, like everything else within the scope of sensation, was utterly without savor. Most distressing of all the instinctual disruptions was that of sleep, along with a complete absence of dreams.

Exhaustion combined with sleeplessness is a rare torture. The two or three hours of sleep I was able to get at night were always at the behest of the Halcion— a matter which deserves particular notice. For some time now many experts in psychopharmacology have warned that the benzodiazepine family of tranquilizers, of which Halcion is one (Valium and Ativan are others), is capable of depressing mood and even precipitating a major depression. Over two years before my siege, an insouciant doctor had prescribed Ativan as a bedtime aid, telling me airily that I could take it as casually as aspirin. The *Physicians' Desk Reference,* the pharmacological bible, reveals that the medicine I had been ingesting was (a) three times the normally prescribed strength, (b) not advisable as a medication for more than a month or so, and (c) to be used with special caution by people of my age. At the time of which I am speaking I was no longer taking Ativan but had become addicted to Halcion and was consuming large doses. It seems reasonable to think that this was still another contributory factor to the trouble that had come upon me. Certainly, it should be a caution to others.

At any rate, my few hours of sleep were usually terminated at three or four in the morning, when I stared up into yawning darkness, wondering and writhing at the devastation taking place in my mind, and awaiting the dawn, which usually permitted me a feverish, dreamless nap. I'm fairly certain that it was during one of these insomniac trances that there came over me the knowledge—a weird and shocking revelation, like that of some long-beshrouded metaphysical truth—that this condition would cost me my life if it continued on such a course. This must have been just before my trip to Paris. Death, as I have said, was now a daily presence, blowing over me in cold gusts. I had not conceived precisely how my end would come. In short, I was still keeping the idea of suicide at bay. But plainly the possibility was around the corner, and I would soon meet it face to face.

What I had begun to discover is that, mysteriously and in ways that are totally remote from normal experience, the gray drizzle of horror induced by depression takes on the quality of physical pain. But it is not an immediately identifiable pain, like that of a broken limb. It may be more accurate to say that despair, owing to some evil trick played upon the sick brain by the inhabiting psyche, comes to resemble the diabolical discomfort of being imprisoned in a fiercely overheated room. And because no breeze stirs this caldron, because there is no escape from this smothering confinement, it is entirely natural that the victim begins to think ceaselessly of oblivion.

V

ONE OF THE MEMORABLE MOMENTS IN *MADAME Bovary* is the scene where the heroine seeks help from the village priest. Guilt-ridden, distraught, miserably depressed, the adulterous Emma—heading toward eventual suicide—stumblingly tries to prod the abbé into helping her find a way out of her misery. But the priest, a simple soul and none too bright, can only pluck at his stained cassock, distractedly shout at his acolytes, and offer Christian platitudes. Emma goes on her quietly frantic way, beyond comfort of God or man.

I felt a bit like Emma Bovary in my relationship with the psychiatrist I shall call Dr. Gold, whom I began to visit immediately after my return from Paris, when the despair had commenced its merciless daily drumming. I had never before consulted a mental therapist for anything, and I felt awkward, also a bit defensive; my pain had become so intense that I considered it quite improbable that conversation with another mortal, even one with professional expertise in mood disorders, could alleviate the distress. Madame Bovary went to the priest with the same hesitant doubt. Yet our society is so structured that Dr. Gold, or someone like him, is the authority to whom one is forced to turn in crisis, and it is not entirely a bad idea, since Dr. Gold—Yale-trained, highly qualified—at least provides a focal point toward which one can direct one's dying energies, offers consolation if not much hope, and becomes the receptacle for an outpouring of woes during fifty minutes that also provides relief for the victim's wife. Still, while I would never question the potential efficacy of psychotherapy in the beginning manifestations or milder forms of the illness—or possibly even in the aftermath of a serious onslaught—its usefulness at the advanced stage I was in has to be virtually nil. My more specific purpose in consulting Dr. Gold was to obtain help through pharmacology—though this too was, alas, a chimera for a bottomed-out victim such as I had become.

He asked me if I was suicidal, and I reluctantly told him yes. I did not particularize—since there seemed no need to—did not tell him that in truth many of the artifacts of my house had become potential devices for my own destruction: the attic rafters (and an outside maple or two) a means to hang myself, the garage a place to inhale carbon monoxide, the bathtub a vessel to receive the flow from my opened arteries. The kitchen knives in their drawers had but one purpose for me. Death by heart attack seemed particularly inviting, absolving me as it would of active responsibility, and I had toyed with the idea of self-induced pneumonia—a long, frigid, shirt-sleeved hike through the rainy woods. Nor had I overlooked an ostensible accident, à la Randall Jarrell, by walking in front of a truck on the highway nearby. These thoughts may seem outlandishly macabre—a strained joke—but they are genuine. They are doubtless especially repugnant to healthy Americans, with their faith in self-improvement. Yet in truth such hideous fantasies, which cause well people to shudder, are to the deeply depressed mind what lascivious daydreams are to persons of robust sexuality. Dr. Gold and I began to chat twice weekly, but there was little I could tell him except to try, vainly, to describe my desolation.

Nor could he say much of value to me. His platitudes were not Christian but, almost as ineffective, dicta drawn straight from the pages of *The Diagnostic and Statistical Manual of the American Psychiatric Association* (much of which, as I mentioned earlier, I'd already read), and the solace he offered me was an antidepressant medication called Ludiomil. The pill made me edgy, disagreeably hyperactive, and when the dosage was increased after ten days, it blocked my bladder for hours one night. Upon informing Dr. Gold of this problem, I was told that ten more days must pass for the drug to clear my system before starting anew with a different pill. Ten days to someone stretched on such a torture rack is like ten centuries— and this does not begin to take into account the fact that when a new pill is inaugurated several weeks must pass before it becomes effective, a development which is far from guaranteed in any case.

This brings up the matter of medication in general. Psychiatry must be given due credit for its continuing struggle to treat depression pharmacologically. The use of lithium to stabilize moods in manic depression is a great medical achievement; the same drug is also being employed effectively as a preventive in many instances of unipolar depression. There can be no doubt that in certain moderate cases and some chronic forms of the disease (the so-called endogenous depressions) medications have proved invaluable, often altering the course of a serious disturbance dramatically. For reasons that are still not clear to me, neither medications nor psychotherapy were able to arrest my plunge toward the depths. If the claims of responsible authorities in the field can be believed—including assertions made by physicians I've come to know personally and to respect—the malign progress of my illness placed me in a distinct minority of patients, severely stricken, whose affliction is beyond control. In any case, I don't want to appear insensitive to the successful treatment ultimately enjoyed by most victims of depression. Especially in its earlier stages, the disease yields favorably to such techniques as cognitive therapy—alone, or in combination with medications—and other continually evolving psychiatric strategies. Most patients, after all, do not need to be hospitalized and do not attempt or actually commit suicide. But until that day when a swiftly acting agent is developed, one's faith in a pharmacological cure for major depression must remain provisional. The failure of these pills to act positively and quickly—a defect which is now the general case—is somewhat analogous to the failure of nearly all drugs to stem massive bacterial infections in the years before antibiotics became a specific remedy. And it can be just as dangerous.

So I found little of worth to anticipate in my consultations with Dr. Gold. On my visits he and I continued to exchange platitudes, mine haltingly spoken now—since my speech, emulating my way of walking, had slowed to the vocal equivalent of a shuffle—and I'm sure as tiresome as his.

Despite the still-faltering methods of treatment, psychiatry has, on an analytical and philosophical level, contributed a lot to an understanding of the origins of depression. Much obviously remains to be learned (and a great deal will doubtless continue to be a mystery, owing to the disease's idiopathic nature, its constant interchangeability of factors), but certainly one psychological element has been established beyond reasonable doubt, and that is the concept of loss. Loss in all of its manifestations is the touchstone of depression—in the progress of the disease and, most likely, in its origin. At a later date I would gradually be persuaded that devastating loss in childhood figured as a probable genesis of my own disorder; meanwhile, as I monitored my retrograde condition, I felt loss at every hand. The loss of self-esteem is a celebrated symptom, and my own sense of self had all but disappeared, along with any self-reliance. This loss can quickly degenerate into dependence, and from dependence into infantile dread. One dreads the loss of all things, all people close and dear. There is an acute fear of abandonment. Being alone in the house, even for a moment, caused me exquisite panic and trepidation.

Of the images recollected from that time the most bizarre and discomfiting remains the one of me, age four and a half, tagging through a market after my long-suffering wife; not for an instant could I let out of my sight the endlessly patient soul who had become nanny, mommy, comforter, priestess, and, most important, confidante—a counselor of rocklike centrality to my existence whose wisdom far exceeded that of Dr. Gold. I would hazard the opinion that many disastrous sequels to depression might be averted if the victims received support such as she gave me. But meanwhile my losses mounted and proliferated. There is no doubt that as one nears the penultimate depths of depression—which is to say just before the stage when one begins to act out one's suicide instead of being a mere contemplator of it—the acute sense of loss is connected with a knowledge of life slipping away at accelerated speed. One develops fierce attachments. Ludicrous things—my reading glasses, a handkerchief, a certain writing instrument—became the objects of my demented possessiveness. Each momentary misplacement filled me with a frenzied dismay, each item being the tactile reminder of a world soon to be obliterated.

November wore on, bleak, raw and chill. One Sunday a photographer and his assistants came to take pictures for an article to be published in a national magazine. Of the session I can recall little except the first snowflakes of winter dotting the air outside. I thought I obeyed the photographer's request to smile often. A day or two later the magazine's editor telephoned my wife, asking if I would submit to another session. The reason he advanced was that the pictures of me, even the ones with smiles, were "too full of anguish."

I had now reached that phase of the disorder where all sense of hope had vanished, along with the idea of a futurity; my brain, in thrall to its outlaw hormones, had become less an organ of thought than an instrument registering, minute by minute, varying degrees of its own suffering. The mornings themselves were becoming bad now as I wandered about lethargic, following my synthetic sleep, but afternoons were still the worst, beginning at about three o'clock, when I'd feel the horror, like some poisonous fogbank, roll in upon my mind, forcing me into bed. There I would lie for as long as six hours, stuporous and virtually paralyzed, gazing at the ceiling and waiting for that moment of evening when, mysteriously, the crucifixion would ease up just enough to allow me to force down some food and then, like an automaton, seek an hour or two of sleep again. Why wasn't I in a hospital?

V I

fOR YEARS I HAD KEPT A NOTEBOOK—NOT STRICTLY a diary, its entries were erratic and haphazardly written—whose contents I would not have particularly liked to be scrutinized by eyes other than my own. I had hidden it well out of sight in my house. I imply no scandalousness; the observations were far less raunchy, or wicked, or self-revealing, than my desire to keep the notebook private might indicate. Nonetheless, the small volume was one that I fully intended to make use of professionally and then destroy before the distant day when the specter of the nursing home came too near. So as my illness worsened I rather queasily realized that if I once decided to get rid of the notebook that moment would necessarily coincide with my decision to put an end to myself. And one evening during early December this moment came.

That afternoon I had been driven (I could no longer drive) to Dr. Gold's office, where he announced that he had decided to place me on the antidepressant Nardil, an older medication which had the advantage of not causing the urinary retention of the other two pills he had prescribed. However, there were drawbacks. Nardil would probably not take effect in less than four to six weeks—I could scarcely believe this—and I would have to carefully obey certain dietary restrictions, fortunately rather epicurean (no sausage, no cheese, no pâté de foie gras), in order to avoid a clash of incompatible enzymes that might cause a stroke. Further, Dr. Gold said with a straight face, the pill at optimum dosage could have the side effect of impotence. Until that moment, although I'd had some trouble with his personality, I had not thought him totally lacking in perspicacity; now I was not at all sure. Putting myself in Dr. Gold's shoes, I wondered if he seriously thought that this juiceless and ravaged semi-invalid with the shuffle and the ancient wheeze woke up each morning from his Halcion sleep eager for carnal fun.

There was a quality so comfortless about that day's session that I went home in a particularly wretched state and prepared for the evening. A few guests were coming over for dinner—something which I neither dreaded nor welcomed and which in itself (that is, in my torpid indifference) reveals a fascinating aspect of depression's pathology. This concerns not the familiar threshold of pain but a parallel phenomenon, and that is the probable inability of the psyche to absorb pain beyond predictable limits of time. There is a region in the experience of pain where the certainty of alleviation often permits superhuman endurance. We learn to live with pain in varying degrees daily, or over longer periods of time, and we are more often than not mercifully free of it. When we endure severe discomfort of a physical nature our conditioning has taught us since childhood to make accommodations to the pain's demands—to accept it, whether pluckily or whimpering and complaining, according to our personal degree of stoicism, but in any case to accept it. Except in intractable terminal pain, there is almost always some form of relief; we look forward to that alleviation, whether it be through sleep or Tylenol or self-hypnosis or a change of posture or, most often, through the body's capacity for healing itself, and we embrace this eventual respite as the natural reward we receive for having been, temporarily, such good sports and doughty sufferers, such optimistic cheerleaders for life at heart.

In depression this faith in deliverance, in ultimate restoration, is absent. The pain is unrelenting, and what makes the condition intolerable is the foreknowledge that no remedy will come—not in a day, an hour, a month, or a minute. If there is mild relief, one knows that it is only temporary; more pain will follow. It is hopelessness even more than pain that crushes the soul. So the decision-making of daily life involves not, as in normal affairs, shifting from one annoying situation to another less annoying—or from discomfort to relative comfort, or from boredom to activity—but moving from pain to pain. One does not abandon, even briefly, one's bed of nails, but is attached to it wherever one goes. And this results in a striking experience—one which I have called, borrowing military terminology, the situation of the walking wounded. For in virtually any other serious sickness, a patient who felt similar devastation would be lying flat in bed, possibly sedated and hooked up to the tubes and wires of life-support systems, but at the very least in a posture of repose and in an isolated setting. His invalidism would be necessary, unquestioned and honorably attained. However, the sufferer from depression has no such option and therefore finds himself, like a walking casualty of war, thrust into the most intolerable social and family situations. There he must, despite the anguish devouring his brain, present a face approximating the one that is associated with ordinary events and companionship. He must try to utter small talk, and be responsive to questions, and knowingly nod and frown and, God help him, even smile. But it is a fierce trial attempting to speak a few simple words.

That December evening, for example, I could have remained in bed as usual during those worst hours, or agreed to the dinner party my wife had arranged downstairs. But the very idea of a decision was academic. Either course was torture, and I chose the dinner not out of any particular merit but through indifference to what I knew would be indistinguishable ordeals of fogbound horror. At dinner I was barely able to speak, but the quartet of guests, who were all good friends, were aware of my condition and politely ignored my catatonic muteness. Then, after dinner, sitting in the living room, I experienced a curious inner convulsion that I can describe only as despair beyond despair. It came out of the cold night; I did not think such anguish possible.

While my friends quietly chatted in front of the fire I excused myself and went upstairs, where I retrieved my notebook from its special place. Then I went to the kitchen and with gleaming clarity—the clarity of one who knows he is engaged in a solemn rite—I noted all the trademarked legends on the well-advertised articles which I began assembling for the volume's disposal: the new roll of Viva paper towels I opened to wrap up the book, the Scotch-brand tape I encircled it with, the empty Post Raisin Bran box I put the parcel into before taking it outside and stuffing it deep down within the garbage can, which would be emptied the next morning. Fire would have destroyed it faster, but in garbage there was an annihilation of self appropriate, as always, to melancholia's fecund self-humiliation. I felt my heart pounding wildly, like that of a man facing a firing squad, and knew I had made an irreversible decision.

A phenomenon that a number of people have noted while in deep depression is the sense of being accompanied by a second self—a wraithlike observer who, not sharing the dementia of his double, is able to watch with dispassionate curiosity as his companion struggles against the oncoming disaster, or decides to embrace it. There is a theatrical quality about all this, and during the next several days, as I went about stolidly preparing for extinction, I couldn't shake off a sense of melodrama—a melodrama in which I, the victim-to-be of self-murder, was both the solitary actor and lone member of the audience. I had not as yet chosen the mode of my departure, but I knew that that step would come next, and soon, as inescapable as nightfall.

I watched myself in mingled terror and fascination as I began to make the necessary preparation: going to see my lawyer in the nearby town—there rewriting my will—and spending part of a couple of afternoons in a muddled attempt to bestow upon posterity a letter of farewell. It turned out that putting together a suicide note, which I felt obsessed with a necessity to compose, was the most difficult task of writing that I had ever tackled. There were too many people to acknowledge, to thank, to bequeath final bouquets. And finally I couldn't manage the sheer dirgelike solemnity of it; there was something I found almost comically offensive in the pomposity of such a comment as "For some time now I have sensed in my work a growing psychosis that is doubtless a reflection of the psychotic strain tainting my life" (this is one of the few lines I recall verbatim), as well as something degrading in the prospect of a testament, which I wished to infuse with at least some dignity and eloquence, reduced to an exhausted stutter of inadequate apologies and self-serving explanations. I should have used as an example

the mordant statement of the Italian writer Cesare
Pavese, who in parting wrote simply: *No more words.
An act. I'll never write again.*

But even a few words came to seem to me too long-
winded, and I tore up all my efforts, resolving to go
out in silence. Late one bitterly cold night, when I
knew that I could not possibly get myself through the
following day, I sat in the living room of the house
bundled up against the chill; something had happened
to the furnace. My wife had gone to bed, and I had
forced myself to watch the tape of a movie in which a
young actress, who had been in a play of mine, was
cast in a small part. At one point in the film, which
was set in late-nineteenth-century Boston, the characters moved down the hallway of a music conservatory,
beyond the walls of which, from unseen musicians,
came a contralto voice, a sudden soaring passage from
the Brahms *Alto Rhapsody*.

This sound, which like all music—indeed, like all
pleasure—I had been numbly unresponsive to for
months, pierced my heart like a dagger, and in a flood
of swift recollection I thought of all the joys the house
had known: the children who had rushed through its
rooms, the festivals, the love and work, the honestly
earned slumber, the voices and the nimble commo-

tion, the perennial tribe of cats and dogs and birds, "laughter and ability and Sighing, / And Frocks and Curls." All this I realized was more than I could ever abandon, even as what I had set out so deliberately to do was more than I could inflict on those memories, and upon those, so close to me, with whom the memories were bound. And just as powerfully I realized I could not commit this desecration on myself. I drew upon some last gleam of sanity to perceive the terrifying dimensions of the mortal predicament I had fallen into. I woke up my wife and soon telephone calls were made. The next day I was admitted to the hospital.

VII

IT WAS DR. GOLD, ACTING AS MY ATTENDING PHYSIcian, who was called in to arrange for my hospital admission. Curiously enough, it was he who told me once or twice during our sessions (and after I had rather hesitantly broached the possibility of hospitalization) that I should try to avoid the hospital at all costs, owing to the stigma I might suffer. Such a comment seemed then, as it does now, extremely misguided; I had thought psychiatry had advanced long beyond the point where stigma was attached to any aspect of mental illness, including the hospital. This refuge, while hardly an enjoyable place, is a facility where patients still may go when pills fail, as they did in my case, and where one's treatment might be regarded as a prolonged extension, in a different setting, of the therapy that begins in offices such as Dr. Gold's.

It's impossible to say, of course, what another doctor's approach might have been, whether he too might have discouraged the hospital route. Many psychiatrists, who simply do not seem to be able to comprehend the nature and depth of the anguish their patients are undergoing, maintain their stubborn allegiance to pharmaceuticals in the belief that eventually the pills will kick in, the patient will respond, and the somber surroundings of the hospital will be avoided. Dr. Gold was such a type, it seems clear, but in my case he was wrong; I'm convinced I should have been in the hospital weeks before. For, in fact, the hospital was my salvation, and it is something of a paradox that in this austere place with its locked and wired doors and desolate green hallways—ambulances screeching night and day ten floors below—I found the repose, the assuagement of the tempest in my brain, that I was unable to find in my quiet farmhouse.

This is partly the result of sequestration, of safety, of being removed to a world in which the urge to pick up a knife and plunge it into one's own breast disappears in the newfound knowledge, quickly apparent even to the depressive's fuzzy brain, that the knife with which he is attempting to cut his dreadful Swiss steak is bendable plastic. But the hospital also offers the mild, oddly gratifying trauma of sudden stabilization— a transfer out of the too familiar surroundings of home, where all is anxiety and discord, into an orderly and benign detention where one's only duty is to try to get well. For me the real healers were seclusion and time.

VIII

THE HOSPITAL WAS A WAY STATION, A PURGATORY. When I entered the place, my depression appeared so profound that, in the opinion of some of the staff, I was a candidate for ECT, electroconvulsive therapy—shock treatment, as it is better known. In many cases this is an effective remedy—it has undergone improvement and has made a respectable comeback, generally shedding the medieval disrepute into which it was once cast—but it is plainly a drastic procedure one would want to avoid. I avoided it because I began to get well, gradually but steadily. I was amazed to discover that the fantasies of self-destruction all but disappeared within a few days after I checked in, and this again is testimony to the pacifying effect that the hospital can create, its immediate value as a sanctuary where peace can return to the mind.

A final cautionary word, however, should be added concerning Halcion. I'm convinced that this tranquilizer is responsible for at least exaggerating to an intolerable point the suicidal ideas that had possessed me before entering the hospital. The empirical evidence that persuades me of this evolves from a conversation I had with a staff psychiatrist only hours after going into the institution. When he asked me what I was taking for sleep, and the dosage, I told him .75 mg of Halcion; at this his face became somber, and he remarked emphatically that this was three times the normally prescribed hypnotic dose, and an amount especially contraindicated for someone my age. I was switched immediately to Dalmane, another hypnotic which is a somewhat longer-acting cousin, and this proved at least as effective as Halcion in putting me to sleep; but most importantly, I noticed that soon after the switch my suicidal notions dwindled then disappeared.

Much evidence has accumulated recently that indicts Halcion (whose chemical name is triazolam) as a causative factor in producing suicidal obsession and other aberrations of thought in susceptible individuals. Because of such reactions Halcion has been categorically banned in the Netherlands, and it should be at least more carefully monitored here. I don't recall Dr. Gold once questioning the overly hefty dose which he knew I was taking; he presumably had not read the warning data in the *Physicians' Desk Reference*. While my own carelessness was at fault in ingesting such an overdose, I ascribe such carelessness to the bland assurance given me several years before, when I began to take Ativan at the behest of the breezy doctor who told me that I could, without harm, take as many of the pills as I wished. One cringes when thinking about the damage such promiscuous prescribing of these potentially dangerous tranquilizers may be creating in patients everywhere. In my case Halcion, of course, was not an independent villain—I was headed for the abyss—but I believe that without it I might not have been brought so low.

I stayed in the hospital for nearly seven weeks. Not everyone might respond the way I did; depression, one must constantly insist, presents so many variations and has so many subtle facets—depends, in short, so much on the individual's totality of causation and response— that one person's panacea might be another's trap. But certainly the hospital (and, of course, I am speaking of the many good ones) should be shorn of its menacing reputation, should not so often be considered the method of treatment of last resort. The hospital is hardly a vacation spot; the one in which I was lodged (I was privileged to be in one of the nation's best) possessed every hospital's stupefying dreariness. If in addition there are assembled on one floor, as on mine, fourteen or fifteen middle-aged males and females in the throes of melancholia of a suicidal complexion, then one can assume a fairly laughterless environment. This was not ameliorated for me by the subairline food or by the peek I had into the outside world: *Dynasty* and *Knots Landing* and the *CBS Evening News* unspooling nightly in the bare recreation room, sometimes making me at least aware that the place where I had found refuge was a kinder, gentler madhouse than the one I'd left. In the hospital I partook of what may be depression's only grudging favor—its ultimate capitulation. Even those for whom any kind of therapy is a futile exercise can look forward to the eventual passing of the storm. If they survive the storm itself, its fury almost always fades and then disappears. Mysterious in its coming, mysterious in its going, the affliction runs its course, and one finds peace.

As I got better I found distraction of sorts in the hospital's routine, with its own institutionalized sitcoms. Group Therapy, I am told, has some value; I would never want to derogate any concept shown to be effective for certain individuals. But Group Therapy did nothing for me except make me seethe, possibly because it was supervised by an odiously smug young shrink, with a spade-shaped dark beard (*der junge Freud?*), who in attempting to get us to cough up the seeds of our misery was alternately condescending and bullying, and occasionally reduced one or two of the women patients, so forlorn in their kimonos and curlers, to what I'm certain he regarded as satisfactory tears. (I thought the rest of the psychiatric staff exemplary in their tact and compassion.) Time hangs heavy

in the hospital, and the best I can say for Group Therapy is that it was a way to occupy the hours.

More or less the same can be said for Art Therapy,
which is organized infantilism. Our class was run by a
delirious young woman with a fixed, indefatigable
smile, who was plainly trained at a school offering
courses in Teaching Art to the Mentally Ill; not even a
teacher of very young retarded children could have
been compelled to bestow, without deliberate instruc-
tion, such orchestrated chuckles and coos. Unwinding
long rolls of slippery mural paper, she would tell us to
take our crayons and make drawings illustrative of
themes that we ourselves had chosen. For example: My
House. In humiliated rage I obeyed, drawing a square,
with a door and four cross-eyed windows, a chimney
on top issuing forth a curlicue of smoke. She showered
me with praise, and as the weeks advanced and my
health improved so did my sense of comedy. I began to
dabble happily in colored modeling clay, sculpting at
first a horrid little green skull with bared teeth, which
our teacher pronounced a splendid replica of my depression. I then proceeded through intermediate stages
of recuperation to a rosy and cherubic head with a
"Have-a-Nice-Day" smile. Coinciding as it did with
the time of my release, this creation truly overjoyed

my instructress (whom I'd become fond of in spite of myself), since, as she told me, it was emblematic of my recovery and therefore but one more example of the triumph over disease by Art Therapy.

By this time it was early February, and although I was still shaky I knew I had emerged into light. I felt myself no longer a husk but a body with some of the body's sweet juices stirring again. I had my first dream in many months, confused but to this day imperishable, with a flute in it somewhere, and a wild goose, and a dancing girl.

I X

By far the great majority of the people who go through even the severest depression survive it, and live ever afterward at least as happily as their unafflicted counterparts. Save for the awfulness of certain memories it leaves, acute depression inflicts few permanent wounds. There is a Sisyphean torment in the fact that a great number—as many as half—of those who are devastated once will be struck again; depression has the habit of recurrence. But most victims live through even these relapses, often coping better because they have become psychologically tuned by past experience to deal with the ogre. It is of great importance that those who are suffering a siege, perhaps for the first time, be told—be convinced, rather—that the illness will run its course and that they will pull through. A tough job, this; calling "Chin up!" from the safety of the shore to a drowning person is tantamount to insult, but it has been shown over and over again that if the encouragement is dogged enough—and the support equally committed and passionate—the endangered one can nearly always be saved. Most people in the grip of depression at its ghastliest are, for whatever reason, in a state of unrealistic hopelessness, torn by exaggerated ills and fatal threats that bear no resemblance to actuality. It may require on the part of friends, lovers, family, admirers, an almost religious devotion to persuade the sufferers of life's worth, which is so often in conflict with a sense of their own worthlessness, but such devotion has prevented countless suicides.

During the same summer of my decline, a close friend of mine—a celebrated newspaper columnist—

was hospitalized for severe manic depression. By the time I had commenced my autumnal plunge my friend had recovered (largely due to lithium but also to psychotherapy in the aftermath), and we were in touch by telephone nearly every day. His support was untiring and priceless. It was he who kept admonishing me that suicide was "unacceptable" (he had been intensely suicidal), and it was also he who made the prospect of going to the hospital less fearsomely intimidating. I still look back on his concern with immense gratitude. The help he gave me, he later said, had been a continuing therapy for him, thus demonstrating that, if nothing else, the disease engenders lasting fellowship.

After I began to recover in the hospital it occurred to me to wonder—for the first time with any really serious concern—why I had been visited by such a calamity. The psychiatric literature on depression is enormous, with theory after theory concerning the disease's etiology proliferating as richly as theories about the death of the dinosaurs or the origin of black holes. The very number of hypotheses is testimony to the malady's all but impenetrable mystery. As for that initial triggering mechanism—what I have called the manifest crisis—can I really be satisfied with the idea that abrupt withdrawal from alcohol started the plunge downward? What about other possibilities—the dour fact, for instance, that at about the same time I was smitten I turned sixty, that hulking milestone of mortality? Or could it be that a vague dissatisfaction with the way in which my work was going—the onset of inertia which has possessed me time and time again during my writing life, and made me crabbed and discontented—had also haunted me more fiercely during that period than ever, somehow magnifying the difficulty with alcohol? Unresolvable questions, perhaps.

These matters in any case interest me less than the search for earlier origins of the disease. What are the forgotten or buried events that suggest an ultimate explanation for the evolution of depression and its later flowering into madness? Until the onslaught of my own illness and its denouement, I never gave much thought to my work in terms of its connection with the subconscious—an area of investigation belonging to literary detectives. But after I had returned to health and was able to reflect on the past in the light of my ordeal, I began to see clearly how depression had clung close to the outer edges of my life for many years. Suicide has been a persistent theme in my books— three of my major characters killed themselves. In re-reading, for the first time in years, sequences from my novels—passages where my heroines have lurched down pathways toward doom—I was stunned to perceive how accurately I had created the landscape of depression in the minds of these young women, describing with what could only be instinct, out of a subconscious already roiled by disturbances of mood, the psychic imbalance that led them to destruction. Thus depression, when it finally came to me, was in fact no stranger, not even a visitor totally unannounced; it had been tapping at my door for decades.

The morbid condition proceeded, I have come to believe, from my beginning years—from my father, who battled the gorgon for much of his lifetime, and had been hospitalized in my boyhood after a despondent spiraling downward that in retrospect I saw greatly resembled mine. The genetic roots of depression seem now to be beyond controversy. But I'm persuaded that an even more significant factor was the death of my mother when I was thirteen; this disorder and early sorrow—the death or disappearance of a parent, especially a mother, before or during puberty—appears repeatedly in the literature on depression as a trauma sometimes likely to create nearly irreparable emotional havoc. The danger is especially apparent if the young person is affected by what has been termed "incomplete mourning"—has, in effect, been unable to achieve the catharsis of grief, and so carries within himself through later years an insufferable burden of which rage and guilt, and not only dammed-up sorrow, are a part, and become the potential seeds of self-destruction.

In an illuminating new book on suicide, *Self-Destruction in the Promised Land,* Howard I. Kushner, who is not a psychiatrist but a social historian, argues persuasively in favor of this theory of incomplete mourning and uses Abraham Lincoln as an example. While Lincoln's hectic moods of melancholy are legend, it is much less well known that in his youth he was often in a suicidal turmoil and came close more than once to making an attempt on his own life. The behavior seems directly linked to the death of Lincoln's mother, Nancy Hanks, when he was nine, and to unexpressed grief exacerbated by his sister's death ten years later. Drawing insights from the chronicle of Lincoln's painful success in avoiding suicide, Kushner makes a convincing case not only for the idea of early loss precipitating self-destructive conduct, but also, auspiciously, for that same behavior becoming a strategy through which the person involved comes to grips with his guilt and rage, and triumphs over self-willed death. Such reconciliation may be entwined with the quest for immortality—in Lincoln's case, no less than that of a writer of fiction, to vanquish death through work honored by posterity.

So if this theory of incomplete mourning has validity, and I think it does, and if it is also true that in the nethermost depths of one's suicidal behavior one is still subconsciously dealing with immense loss while trying to surmount all the effects of its devastation, then my own avoidance of death may have been belated homage to my mother. I do know that in those last hours before I rescued myself, when I listened to the passage from the *Alto Rhapsody*—which I'd heard her sing— she had been very much on my mind.

X

NEAR THE END OF AN EARLY FILM OF INGMAR BERGman's, *Through a Glass Darkly,* a young woman, experiencing the embrace of what appears to be profound psychotic depression, has a terrifying hallucination. Anticipating the arrival of some transcendental and saving glimpse of God, she sees instead the quivering shape of a monstrous spider that is attempting to violate her sexually. It is an instant of horror and scalding truth. Yet even in this vision of Bergman (who has suffered cruelly from depression) there is a sense that all of his accomplished artistry has somehow fallen short of a true rendition of the drowned mind's appalling phantasmagoria. Since antiquity—in the tortured lament of Job, in the choruses of Sophocles and Aeschylus—chroniclers of the human spirit have been wrestling with a vocabulary that might give proper expression to the desolation of melancholia. Through the course of literature and art the theme of depression has run like a durable thread of woe—from Hamlet's soliloquy to the verses of Emily Dickinson and Gerard Manley Hopkins, from John Donne to Hawthorne and Dostoevski and Poe, Camus and Conrad and Virginia Woolf. In many of Albrecht Dürer's engravings there are harrowing depictions of his own melancholia; the manic wheeling stars of Van Gogh are the precursors of the artist's plunge into dementia and the extinction of self. It is a suffering that often tinges the music of Beethoven, of Schumann and Mahler, and permeates the darker cantatas of Bach. The vast metaphor which most faithfully represents this fathomless ordeal, how-

ever, is that of Dante, and his all-too-familiar lines
still arrest the imagination with their augury of the
unknowable, the black struggle to come:

> *Nel mezzo del cammin di nostra vita*
> *Mi ritrovai per una selva oscura,*
> *Ché la diritta via era smarrita.*

> *In the middle of the journey of our life*
> *I found myself in a dark wood,*
> *For I had lost the right path.*

One can be sure that these words have been more
than once employed to conjure the ravages of melancholia, but their somber foreboding has often over-
shadowed the last lines of the best-known part of that
poem, with their evocation of hope. To most of those
who have experienced it, the horror of depression is so
overwhelming as to be quite beyond expression, hence
the frustrated sense of inadequacy found in the work of
even the greatest artists. But in science and art the
search will doubtless go on for a clear representation of
its meaning, which sometimes, for those who have
known it, is a simulacrum of all the evil of our world:
of our everyday discord and chaos, our irrationality,
warfare and crime, torture and violence, our impulse

toward death and our flight from it held in the intolerable equipoise of history. If our lives had no other configuration but this, we should want, and perhaps deserve, to perish; if depression had no termination, then suicide would, indeed, be the only remedy. But one need not sound the false or inspirational note to stress the truth that depression is not the soul's annihilation; men and women who have recovered from the disease—and they are countless—bear witness to what is probably its only saving grace: it is conquerable.

For those who have dwelt in depression's dark wood, and known its inexplicable agony, their return from the abyss is not unlike the ascent of the poet, trudging upward and upward out of hell's black depths and at last emerging into what he saw as "the shining world." There, whoever has been restored to health has almost always been restored to the capacity for serenity and joy, and this may be indemnity enough for having endured the despair beyond despair.

E quindi uscimmo a riveder le stelle.

And so we came forth, and once again beheld the stars.